WOULD YOU RATHER?...

Over 300 CRAZY QUESTIONS plus extra pages to make up your own!

DOUBLY DISGUSTING

Justin Heimberg & David Gomberg

Published by Seven Footer Press
247 West 30th St., 11th Fl.
New York, NY 10001
First Printing, October 2009
10 9 8 7 6 5 4 3 2
Manufactured in Baltimore, Maryland, October 2009

Would You Rather...?® is a registered trademark used under license from
Falls Media LLC, an Imagination company.

Design by Thomas Schirtz

ISBN 978-1-934734-00-1

www.sevenfooterpress.com

Table of Contents

Disgusting! 1

You've Been Cursed 21

Powers and Fantasies 49

Cool and Unusual Punishments 77

Doubly Disgusting 99

Would You Rather Live in a World Where... 119

Would You... 137

Getting Personal 153

Doubly Doubly Disgusting 169

Random Play 193

Make Your Own Questions! 209

HOW TO USE THIS BOOK

1. Sit around with a bunch of friends.

2. Read a question from the book out loud and talk about it.

   You won't believe some of the stuff you'll come up with as you think about which choice to make.

3. Everybody must choose! That's the whole point. It forces you to really think about the options.

4. Once everyone has chosen, move on to the next question.

It's that simple. We have provided a few things to think about for each question, but don't stop there. Much of the fun comes from imagining the different ways your choice will affect your life. You may want to grab a pencil, as sometimes, you will get to fill in the blank with the name of someone you know or other information. Other times, you will make up your own questions, keep score of who chose what, and more! Enough jibber-jabber. It's time to enter the demented world of *Would You Rather...?*

CHAPTER ONE

Disgusting!

You asked for disgusting, and you got it. Concerning all things nasty, vile, and just plain gross, these sick questions will hit you like a rainstorm of boogers. Each question offers two possible fates, each delightfully more disgusting than the next. Choose wisely.

Would you rather...

step in dog doo every fifth step you take

OR

get hit with bird poo every thirty seconds?

Would you rather...

produce 100 times the amount of saliva you currently produce

OR

produce 100 times the boogers you currently produce?

YOU MUST CHOOSE!

Would you rather...

sleep nightly in a bed of worms

OR

bathe daily in a tub filled with daddy longlegs spiders?

Would you rather...

retrieve a marble at the bottom of a barrel of thumbtacks

OR

at the bottom of a barrel of cockroaches?

Take a vote!

Number of people who voted for **choice #1**:.........

Number of people who voted for **choice #2**:.........

YOU MUST CHOOSE!

WOULD YOU RATHER...LICK AN ICE CREAM CONE COVERED IN ANTS

OR EAT A HOT DOG SMOTHERED IN CATERPILLAR GUTS?

Would you rather...

eat a peanut butter and jellyfish sandwich

OR

a ham and toe cheese (the gunk between your toes) sandwich?

Would you rather...

toss a handful of walnuts into your mouth, only to discover that they were actually beetles

OR

chew on a piece of bubble gum, only to discover that you were actually chewing on a live baby squid?

YOU MUST CHOOSE!

Would you rather...

gargle a mouthful of dog slobber

OR

eat a plate of earthworm spaghetti?

Take a vote!

Number of people who voted for **choice #1**:………

Number of people who voted for **choice #2**:………

YOU MUST CHOOSE!

Would you rather...

laugh so hard that milk comes out of your nose and then have to drink it

OR

be fed regurgitated food by your mom like mother birds feed their chicks?

Would you rather...

have nose hair that touches the ground

OR

armpit hair that touches the ground?

YOU MUST CHOOSE!

Would you rather...

have to trim the toenails and fingernails of your entire class by biting them

OR

drink two glasses worth of milk straight from the udder of a goat?

Would you rather...

have a permanent paper cut between your fingers

OR

a permanent canker sore in your mouth?

YOU MUST CHOOSE!

Would you rather...

sneeze moths

OR

cough up tiny frogs?

Would you rather...

eat salmon-flavored ice cream with salmon chunks **OR** bubble gum ice cream full of already chewed gum wads?

broccoli-flavored ice cream **OR** Centipedes N' Cream?

Ground Beef Sherbet **OR** Lima Bean Sorbet?

What's the most disgusting flavor you can come up with?

YOU MUST CHOOSE!

Would you rather...

eat a chocolate chip cookie where the chips are flies

OR

consume a jelly donut where the jelly is snot?

Reasons **1st choice** is better

....
....
....
....
....

Reasons **2nd choice** is better

....
....
....
....
....

YOU MUST CHOOSE!

Would you rather...

constantly sweat but always smell good

OR

never sweat at all but always smell like a wet dog?

Would you rather...

grow an extra one-inch layer of flesh for every year of your life like a tree grows wood

OR

shed your skin and hair every autumn?

YOU MUST CHOOSE!

Would you rather...

have a runny nose that won't quit for a month

OR

a bloody nose that won't quit for a day?

Who chose what and why...

Name _____ Choice _____

Why _____

Name _____ Choice _____

Why _____

Name _____ Choice _____

Why _____

YOU MUST CHOOSE!

Would you rather...

lick an ashtray **OR** a pig's lips?

the floor of your school cafeteria **OR** the floor of a barber shop?

the bottom of your friend's foot **OR** the top of a termite mound?

Would you rather...

have to drink a warm glass of sweat each morning

OR

have to eat a larva grub each morning rather than a daily vitamin?

YOU MUST CHOOSE!

Make Your Own "DISGUSTING" Question!

Make up **two choices** that are **equally disgusting**!

Would you rather...

_____

_____

OR

_____

_____?

Who chose what and why...

Name _____ Choice _____

Why _____

Name _____ Choice _____

Why _____

Name _____ Choice _____

Why _____

Would you rather...

go down a water slide of mucus

OR

through a Slip 'n Slide of horse manure?

Would you rather...

get a zit on your tongue **OR** your eyeball?

in your nostril **OR** right in the center of your forehead?

a zit the size of a marble on the tip of your nose **OR** the size of a golf ball on the bottom of your chin?

YOU MUST CHOOSE!

Would you rather...

have to brush your teeth with a used toilet scrub brush

OR

wash your hair with a bottle of bird poo?

Would you rather...

your eyelids were permanently flipped inside out

OR

be permanently cross-eyed?

YOU MUST CHOOSE!

Would you rather...

have unlimited text-messaging

OR

permission for unlimited farting?

YOU MUST CHOOSE!

CHAPTER TWO

You've Been Cursed

Unlucky you. It seems that the fates have decided to complicate your life in a most bizarre way. You are to suffer a strange curse that will change your life forever (and not for the better). Well, at least you'll have some say in the matter, since you get to choose between two equally horrific choices.

Would you rather...

always talk like you do when you're holding your nose

OR

talk like you do when you're gargling water?

Would you rather...

have a permanent wind blowing in your face

OR

permanent fingerpaint on your hands?

YOU MUST CHOOSE!

Would you rather...

snore the sound of a tuba

OR

snore with the power of a vacuum?

Would you rather...

be full of holes like Swiss cheese

OR

have suction cups all over your body like an octopus?

YOU MUST CHOOSE!

Would you rather...

have to clean yourself like a cat

OR

have to use a litter box like a cat?

Would you rather...

blink 1,000 times per minute

OR

be unable to ever shut your eyes?

YOU MUST CHOOSE!

Would you rather...

share your house with three of your teachers

OR

have to go to school seven days a week?

Would you rather...

only be able to travel on airplanes while riding inside an oversized pet carrier

OR

be limited to wearing either pants or a shirt, but never both at the same time?

YOU MUST CHOOSE!

Would you rather...

have a horse's tail **OR** a baboon's butt?

a pig's snout for a nose **OR** a rooster's wattle under your chin (the fleshy piece of skin hanging under the beak)?

reindeer antlers sprouting from the top of your head **OR** a rhino horn jutting out from the front of your face?

Would you rather...

talk at six times normal speed

OR

one-third normal speed?

YOU MUST CHOOSE!

Would you rather...

have a crazy straw for an outie belly button

OR

have shoelaces for eyelashes?

Would you rather...

when passing by people on the street, be compelled to guard them as if playing basketball

OR

feel the urge to stuff acorns in your cheeks like squirrels do?

YOU MUST CHOOSE!

Would you rather...

only be able to eat garnish to survive

OR

only be able to eat food that begins with the letter "y"?

Would you rather...

have tin foil skin **OR** bones made of solid iron?

a Slinky for your neck **OR** hockey sticks for your legs?

coffee mugs for hands **OR** chopsticks for fingers?

YOU MUST CHOOSE!

Would you rather...

sleep every other hour

OR

every other day?

Who chose what and why...

Name _____ Choice _____

Why _____

Name _____ Choice _____

Why _____

Name _____ Choice _____

Why _____

YOU MUST CHOOSE!

Would you rather...

have a vertical mouth

OR

vertical eyes?

Would you rather...

your teachers speak in Dr. Seuss rhymes

OR

in rap?

YOU MUST CHOOSE!

Would you rather...

have a perpetual watch glint shining in your eyes

OR

a constant itch on your back that you can't reach?

Would you rather...

have a belly button that rings like a doorbell when pushed

OR

one that has a Magic 8-Ball readout in it?

YOU MUST CHOOSE!

Would you rather...

wake up each day with a new hair color and style

OR

a new last name?

Take a vote!

Number of people who voted for choice #1:.........

Number of people who voted for choice #2:.........

Would you rather...

have the face of an 80-year-old

OR

the face of a 2-year-old?

YOU MUST CHOOSE!

Make Your Own "YOU'VE BEEN CURSED" Question!
Make up two choices that are equally weird!

Would you rather...

_____

_____

OR

_____

_____?

Who chose what and why...

Name _____ Choice _____

Why _____

Name _____ Choice _____

Why _____

Name _____ Choice _____

Why _____

Would you rather...

fart laughing gas

OR

cry chocolate syrup?

Reasons *1st* **choice** is better

....
....
....
....
....

Reasons *2nd* **choice** is better

....
....
....
....
....

Would you rather...

have a bed that flips you out to wake you in the morning

OR

one that heats up?

YOU MUST CHOOSE!

Would you rather...

neigh like a horse when you get upset

OR

howl like a coyote when you're excited?

Would you rather...

have the neck of a 90-year-old

OR

have the feet of a 90-year-old?

YOU MUST CHOOSE!

Would you rather...

have to get everywhere by riding a Big Wheel

OR

by using a hippity hop ball?

Would you rather...

have staplers for feet

OR

paintbrushes for fingers?

YOU MUST CHOOSE!

Would you rather...

always have a limb asleep

OR

yawn uncontrollably from 10 to 2 every day?

Would you rather...

be raised by dogs **OR** chimps?

be raised by angels **OR** the Harlem Globetrotters?

be raised by 5-year-olds **OR** the Jonas Brothers?

YOU MUST CHOOSE!

Would you rather...

be unable to distinguish between sinks and toilets

OR

pillows and beehives?

Would you rather...

never be able to save an e-mail

OR

a picture?

YOU MUST CHOOSE!

Would you rather...

have to write without using vowels

OR

without using consonants?

Would you rather...

produce caramel under your arms when sweating

OR

have hot sauce for saliva?

YOU MUST CHOOSE!

Would you rather...

talk like Donald Trump

OR

have his hair?

Would you rather...

be tethered to your home by a 200-foot cord

OR

become as light as helium when the sun goes down?

YOU MUST CHOOSE!

Would you rather...

all your weight go to your thighs **OR** to your butt?

to your stomach **OR** to your ankles and upper arms?

to your neck **OR** to your forehead?

Would you rather...

have broccoli for hair

OR

forks for hands?

YOU MUST CHOOSE!

Would you rather...

have foot long eyelashes

OR

have nose hair that connects from one nostril to the other?

Would you rather...

have to still use a bib **OR** a car seat?

a bottle **OR** diapers?

a stroller **OR** a high chair?

YOU MUST CHOOSE!

Would you rather...

have a Mohawk

OR

have your current hair except with your name shaved in the back of your head?

Would you rather...

always feel like you do when you eat too much

OR

always feel like you've got to go number one?

YOU MUST CHOOSE!

Would you rather...

your school bag weigh 50 lbs.

OR

only be able to write using crayons?

Take a vote!

Number of people who voted for **choice #1**:.........

Number of people who voted for **choice #2**:.........

YOU MUST CHOOSE!

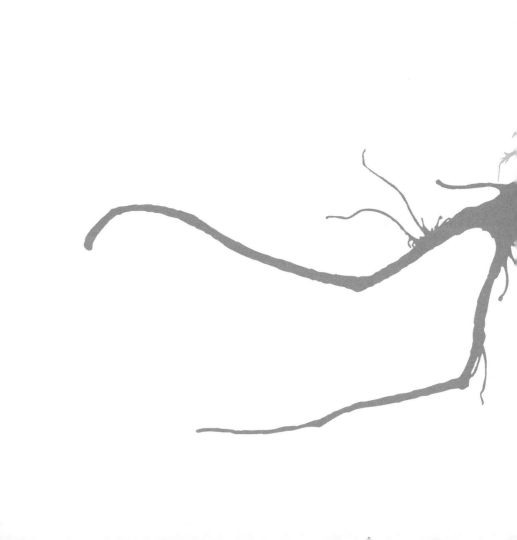

CHAPTER THREE

POWERS AND FANTASIES

It's your lucky day. You are about to be blessed with a magical superpower to rival Superman, Spider-Man, and Iron Man. Even better, you have a say in the matter. You get to choose between two options.

Would you rather...

have a pencil that magically answers
all math questions correctly

OR

a fielder's mitt that magically catches
all fly balls?

Would you rather...

be able to dry yourself after showering by shaking your
hair like a wet dog

OR

have self-combing hair?

YOU MUST CHOOSE!

Would you rather...

be able to remember every second of your life
from the time you were born

OR

not remember anything other than the last day but
know precisely what will happen to you in the future?

Reasons *1st choice* is better

....

....

....

....

....

Reasons *2nd choice* is better

....

....

....

....

....

YOU MUST CHOOSE!

51

Would you rather...

be able to correctly identify the person who farted with 100% accuracy

OR

have the ability to use your snot as Krazy Glue?

Would you rather...

have a visor that can slide in and out of your forehead

OR

have Heelys built into the bottoms of your feet?

YOU MUST CHOOSE!

Would you rather...

be able to dispense salt and pepper out of your nostrils

OR

be able to burp the smell of roses?

Would you rather...

have a Nerf lawn

OR

have beanbag bushes?

YOU MUST CHOOSE!

Would you rather...

have extra eyeballs in the palms of your hands

OR

not?

Would you rather...

your family be secret agents

OR

a world-famous band?

YOU MUST CHOOSE!

Would you rather...

live near a pond of hot fudge

OR

a mountain of ice cream?

Would you rather...

be able to answer any teacher's question when called on,
but only if you used a phony French accent

OR

be able to solve any math problem,
but only while barefoot?

YOU MUST CHOOSE!

57

Would you rather...

live in the White House

OR

an amusement park?

Would you... accept the power to be able to fly in exchange for weighing 500 pounds?

YOU MUST CHOOSE!

WOULD YOU RATHER...
HAVE FINGERS THAT FUNCTION AS SCISSORS

OR A BELLY BUTTON THAT FUNCTIONS AS A HOT CHOCOLATE MACHINE?

59

Would you rather...

play a game of basketball with your favorite player

OR

play this book with the President?

Would you rather...

live in the world of your favorite video game

OR

your favorite movie?

YOU MUST CHOOSE!

WOULD YOU RATHER...BE ABLE TO SHOOT RUBBER BANDS 100 FEET WITH PINPOINT ACCURACY

TWANG! - - - - - P-YOW!

OR BE ABLE TO SET THE TABLE WITH YOUR MIND?

Would you rather...

own a self-making bed

OR

a self-emptying trash can?

Would you rather...

have the power to instantly thaw frozen food by dropping it down your pants

OR

be able to exterminate roaches by breathing on them?

YOU MUST CHOOSE!

Would you rather...

have a sandpaper tongue

OR

switchblade fingernails?

Would you rather...

be reincarnated as a rabbit

OR

a snake?

YOU MUST CHOOSE!

If you were the commissioner of Major League Baseball,

Would you rather...

the pitcher's mound be 12 feet high

OR

the baseball diamond's dirt be covered in freshly laid wet cement?

Would you rather...

the outfield wall be covered in poison ivy

OR

the warning track be filled with quicksand?

What other changes can you think of that would make baseball more exciting?

YOU MUST CHOOSE!

Would you rather...

your dreams were written by JK Rowling

OR

the writers of *Lost*?

Would you rather...

never miss a basketball free throw

OR

be able to type your thoughts by resting your head on your computer keyboard?

YOU MUST CHOOSE!

Would you rather...

have chocolate boogers

OR

strawberry-flavored toe gunk?

Would you rather...

be able to pop popcorn kernels in your closed fist

OR

be able to make real sounds when playing air guitar?

YOU MUST CHOOSE!

Would you rather...

have a daily allowance of 10,000 calories with no weight gain

OR

have the ability to give instant and intense diarrhea to anyone you wish?

Would you rather...

have sugar dandruff

OR

sunflower seed warts?

YOU MUST CHOOSE!

Would you rather...

have perfect aim with spitballs

OR

be able to shoot pencils with your belly fat with the force and accuracy of a bow and arrow?

Would you rather...

trade lives with Conan O'Brien

OR

Tiger Woods?

YOU MUST CHOOSE!

Would you rather...

have a panther that obeys your every command and does your bidding

OR

500 bees that do the same?

YOU MUST CHOOSE!

WOULD YOU RATHER...
HAVE A FROG TONGUE

OR A KANGAROO POUCH?

Would you rather...

be able to fly, but only see in black-and-white

OR

be able to become invisible, but lose the ability to smell and taste?

YOU MUST CHOOSE!

Would you rather...

have the power to know exactly which questions will appear on your tests

OR

have the ability to read the mind of any cat?

Take a vote!

Number of people who voted for **choice #1**:.........

Number of people who voted for **choice #2**:.........

YOU MUST CHOOSE!

Would you rather...

have nostrils that function as a jetpack

OR

make poops that smell like oranges?

Take a vote!

Number of people who voted for **choice #1**:.........

Number of people who voted for **choice #2**:.........

YOU MUST CHOOSE!

Would you rather...

have LeBron James' dunking skills but permanent, incurable body odor

OR

Tom Brady's passing arm, but permanent, incurable poison ivy on both ankles?

Who chose what and why...

Name _____ Choice _____

Why _____

Name _____ Choice _____

Why _____

Name _____ Choice _____

Why _____

YOU MUST CHOOSE!

CHAPTER FOUR

COOL AND UNUSUAL PUNISHMENTS

Uh oh. You must have been misbehaving. Because the fates have decided that you must suffer a horrible experience—a painful challenge, an embarrassing moment, or something else horrific, disgusting, or just generally unpleasant.

Would you rather...

use boiling water eye drops

OR

gargle Tabasco sauce?

Would you rather...

have to wash your mouth out with soap every time you say the word "the"

OR

share your bed nightly with a family of raccoons?

YOU MUST CHOOSE!

Would you rather...

have ten bees fly up your nose

OR

swallow ten live wasps?

Reasons **1ˢᵗ choice** is better

....

....

....

....

Reasons **2ⁿᵈ choice** is better

....

....

....

....

YOU MUST CHOOSE!

Would you rather...

have to spend a ten hour car ride with the most annoying kid in school

OR

the meanest teacher in school?

Would you rather...

get bombarded with snot rockets

OR

have a bunch of baseball players spit tobacco on you?

YOU MUST CHOOSE!

Would you rather...

have to wear the same pair of underwear until you turn 40 years old

OR

be stuck attending nursery school until then?

Take a vote!

Number of people who voted for choice #1:.........

Number of people who voted for choice #2:.........

YOU MUST CHOOSE!

Would you rather...

have hangnails that are two inches long

OR

have an ingrown toenail that can never be cut and grows inside your leg?

Would you rather...

have everyone stick their gum on you when done chewing

OR

have everyone use your shirt as a handkerchief?

YOU MUST CHOOSE!

Would you rather...

have 100 mosquito bites on the inside of your mouth

OR

get poison ivy on the inside of your eyelids?

Would you rather take your showers...

in scalding hot water **OR** ice cold water?

hot fudge **OR** Marshmallow Fluff?

nasal drip **OR** a stranger's sweat?

YOU MUST CHOOSE!

Would you rather...

only be able to drink from water fountains

OR

only be able to eat from vending machines?

Would you rather...

sleep on a pillow covered in porcupine quills

OR

with a blanket constructed out of live garter snakes?

YOU MUST CHOOSE!

Would you rather...

bungee jump off a cliff with the cord attached to your ears

OR

your tongue?

Would you rather...

never get a birthday present

OR

get presents, but always have to invite all your friends and classmates to a party planned to please a 4-year-old girl?

YOU MUST CHOOSE!

WOULD YOU RATHER...
YOUR LITTLE BROTHER HAVE THE ABILITY TO DIRECT YOUR MOVEMENTS USING A NINTENDO WII CONTROLLER

OR HAVE TO ALWAYS STUFF YOUR PANTS WITH HERMIT CRABS BEFORE LEAVING YOUR HOUSE?

Would you rather...

be the only one the teacher calls on in any of your classes

OR

be responsible for doing the homework for everyone in your classes?

Would you rather...

jump into a pool of piranhas

OR

a pit of rattlesnakes?

YOU MUST CHOOSE!

89

Would you rather...

always have to dress like an Egyptian pharaoh **OR** a Revolutionary War soldier?

a professional hockey player **OR** a chef?

Fred Flintstone **OR** Buzz Lightyear?

If you had to wear one outfit for the rest of your life, what would it be? ....

YOU MUST CHOOSE!

Would you rather...

be a window washer for the top of the
Empire State Building

OR

an underground sewer cleaner?

Take a vote!

Number of people who voted for **choice #1**:.........

Number of people who voted for **choice #2**:.........

YOU MUST CHOOSE!

WOULD YOU RATHER... WEAR A WASP NEST AS A HAT

OR A WEAR A KING COBRA AS A TIE?

92

Would you rather...

watch your dad belly dance

OR

listen to your mom sing in front of the whole school?

Would you rather share your house...

with five pigs **OR** five clowns?

a mime **OR** a crow?

12 Spanish soccer announcers **OR** 100 St. Bernards?

YOU MUST CHOOSE!

Would you rather...

get caught in an avalanche of boogers

OR

a tidal wave of vomit?

Who chose what and why...

Name _____ Choice _____

Why _____

Name _____ Choice _____

Why _____

Name _____ Choice _____

Why _____

YOU MUST CHOOSE!

Would you rather...

not be allowed to use your hands when you eat

OR

not be allowed to sleep lying down?

YOU MUST CHOOSE!

Would you rather...

wear a shirt full of itching powder

OR

socks filled with angry fire ants?

Would you rather...

have all your eyelashes plucked out

OR

rub rough sandpaper over your recently scraped knee?

YOU MUST CHOOSE!

CHAPTER FIVE

DOUBLY DISGUSTING

Just when you thought it was safe to eat comes another chapter about the downright dirty and disgusting. Once again, you are given a choice between two possible fates, each more ridiculously revolting than the next. So what exactly is *doubly* disgusting? You're about to find out.

Would you rather...

have boogers that crawled out of your nose whenever they wanted **OR** boogers the size and shape of dice?

glow-in-the-dark boogers **OR** mood boogers (their color changes depending on your mood)?

helium-filled boogers **OR** boogers that function as Party Snaps (when you toss them on the ground they make small explosion noises)?

YOU MUST CHOOSE!

Would you rather...

bite off a stranger's warts

OR

tongue-wash hair that hasn't been washed in a week?

Who chose what and why...

Name _____ Choice _____

Why _____

Name _____ Choice _____

Why _____

Name _____ Choice _____

Why _____

YOU MUST CHOOSE!

WOULD YOU RATHER...HAVE A MILLIPEDE CRAWL UP ONE NOSTRIL AND OUT THE OTHER

OR HAVE A BABY BAT FLY INTO YOUR MOUTH?

Would you rather...

have see-through skin

OR

eyes that dangle from their sockets (but are functional)?

Take a vote!

Number of people who voted for **choice** #1:.........

Number of people who voted for **choice** #2:.........

YOU MUST CHOOSE!

Would you rather...

have the world record for the longest tongue **OR** the most ear hair?

the hairiest back **OR** the thickest neck?

for making the largest poop **OR** having the worst body odor?

Would you rather...

eat 20 sticks of butter

OR

an entire bag of flour?

YOU MUST CHOOSE!

WOULD YOU RATHER...
DRINK STRAIGHT FROM A COW'S UDDER

OR EAT A BLOCK OF 20 YEAR OLD MOLDY CHEESE?

Would you rather...

drool creamed spinach

OR

have a pimento (that red thing in olives) in each nostril?

Would you rather...

have a stomach that constantly growls as loud as a lion

OR

a nose that throbs like a human heart?

Reasons *1st choice* is better

....

....

....

Reasons *2nd choice* is better

....

....

....

YOU MUST CHOOSE!

Would you rather...

have to drink a flounder milkshake

OR

a meatloaf-flavored sports drink?

Would you rather...

only be able to bathe using a single bathtub full of water which you need to share with your family for an entire year

OR

be locked in a room filled with 100,000 horseflies for one day?

YOU MUST CHOOSE!

Would you rather...

eat a fingernail sandwich

OR

have to tongue-clean the holes of a used bowling ball?

Would you rather...

stick a straw up a friend's nostril and slurp hard

OR

lick the eyeballs of the next 10 people you meet?

YOU MUST CHOOSE!

Would you rather...

have cankles (no distinction between your calves and your ankles)

OR

a nin (no distinction between your neck and your chin)?

Would you rather......

have your teeth surgically removed and replaced with golf tees **OR** marshmallows?

maggots **OR** tufts of hair?

Make Up Your Own:

_____

OR

_____ ?

YOU MUST CHOOSE!

Would you rather...

be eating a salad and find a long, long hair in your mouth

OR

be licking a Tootsie Pop, only to find a roach
in the middle?

Reasons *1st choice* is better

....
....
....
....
....

Reasons *2nd choice* is better

....
....
....
....
....

Would you rather...

have ants crawling under your skin

OR

have a moth living in your mouth?

YOU MUST CHOOSE!

WOULD YOU RATHER... HAVE A SPINNING PROPELLER ATTACHED TO THE TOP OF YOUR HEAD

BUZZzzzz

OR BE CONSTANTLY COVERED IN A LAYER OF FILTH LIKE PIG-PEN FROM CHARLIE BROWN?

COUGH

HACK!

Would you rather...

have an ant burrow into your ear drum
and lay hundreds of eggs

OR

a collection of wasps make your nose
their nest?

Take a vote!

Number of people who voted for **choice #1**:.........

Number of people who voted for **choice #2**:.........

YOU MUST CHOOSE!

Would you rather...

all your clothing be made from human hair

OR

baby rats?

Would you rather...

have pimples that pop with the sound and force of a firecracker

OR

ear hair that grows one foot per day?

YOU MUST CHOOSE!

Make Your Own "Doubly *DISGUSTING*" Question!
Make up **two choices** that are **equally disgusting!**

Would you rather...

_____

_____

OR

_____

_____ ?

Reasons *1st* **choice** is better

Reasons *2nd* **choice** is better

114

Would you rather...

have a comb-over from your eye-lashes

OR

ear hair?

Would you rather...

vomit up dirt **OR** Crayola crayons?

marbles **OR** dice?

lightning bugs **OR** butterflies?

YOU MUST CHOOSE!

Would you rather...

have caramel ear wax

OR

hot fudge snot?

Would you rather...

have the eyes of a fly

OR

be covered from head to toe in the scales of a fish?

YOU MUST CHOOSE!

WOULD YOU RATHER...
HAVE RAZOR SHARP QUILLS INSTEAD OF HAIR

HUG

HUG

OR ARMS TWICE AS LONG AS YOUR BODY?

CHAPTER SIX

WOULD YOU RATHER LIVE IN A WORLD WHERE...

The world is a crazy place. But not crazy enough. The laws of nature are about to be turned upside-down. And the best part is, you get a say in the matter.

WOULD YOU RATHER...
LIVE IN A WORLD WHERE EVERYTHING,
INCLUDING PEOPLE, WAS MADE
OUT OF MARSHMALLOW

OR WHERE THE MAIN FORM OF TRANSPORTATION
WAS BUMPER CARS?

BUMPERVILLE
NEXT EXIT →

BUMP!

Would you rather live in a world where...

people could breathe underwater

OR

where animals could speak?

Take a vote!

Number of people who voted for **choice #1**:.........

Number of people who voted for **choice #2**:.........

Would you rather live in a world where...

it rained Kool-Aid

OR

where it snowed cotton candy?

YOU MUST CHOOSE!

121

Would you rather live in a world where...

instead of shaking hands, people slapped each other

OR

where people got around by gymnastic floor exercise routines?

Would you rather live in a world where...

there was no gravity

OR

where gravity was twice as strong as normal? What would life be like?

YOU MUST CHOOSE!

Would you rather live in a world where...

our echoes had French accents

OR

our echoes sound two seconds before we spoke?

Would you rather live in a world where...

kids were the teachers and adults were the students

OR

not?
What would you teach the grown-ups?

YOU MUST CHOOSE!

Would you rather live in a world without...

soap **OR** pizza?

telephones **OR** sports?

pants **OR** the Internet?

What are 5 things you could never live without:

1
2
3
4
5

YOU MUST CHOOSE!

Would you rather live in a world where...

everybody's speech was badly dubbed over
like in a kung-fu movie

OR

where all arguments were settled
by means of break-dancing contests?

YOU MUST CHOOSE!

125

Would you rather live in a world where...

you could change your name every day

OR

where you could change your height by making the pitch of your voice higher or lower?

Who chose what and why...

Name _____ Choice _____
Why _____
Name _____ Choice _____
Why _____
Name _____ Choice _____
Why _____

YOU MUST CHOOSE!

Would you rather live in a world where...

police washed mouths out with soap and issued spankings and time-outs for criminal offenses

OR

where traffic lights changed from green to red and back again every five seconds?

YOU MUST CHOOSE!

Would you rather live in a world where...

Transformers were real

OR

the characters from *Dragon Tales* were?

Would you rather live in a world where...

no friendship lasted longer than a week

OR

where you could only remember ten people at a time?

YOU MUST CHOOSE!

Would you rather live in a world where...

all air smelled like tuna fish

OR

all water tasted like cheese?

Would you rather live in a world where...

we aged backwards

OR

not?

YOU MUST CHOOSE!

Would you rather live in a world where...

Thursdays lasted 96 hours

OR

all food was consumed in liquid form?

Reasons *1st choice* is better

....
....
....
....
....

Reasons *2nd choice* is better

....
....
....
....

YOU MUST CHOOSE!

131

Would you rather live in a world where...

people had multiple lives like in a video game

OR

we had robots to help around the house?

Would you rather live in a world where...

dinosaurs still roamed the earth

OR

where Barney was a common species of creature that lived in the wild?

YOU MUST CHOOSE!

Would you rather live in a world without...

TV **OR** texting?

punctuation **OR** glass?

MTV **OR** McDonalds?

Would you rather live in a world where...

whoever denied it supplied it

OR

whoever smelt it dealt it?

YOU MUST CHOOSE!

133

Would you rather live in a world where...

kids get to sing on stage with their favorite band

OR

where they get to play with their favorite sports team?

YOU MUST CHOOSE!

Would you rather live in a world where...

you could rewind your life

OR

fast-forward it?

Would you rather live in...

a giant card house **OR** a house of glass?

a house of moonbounce material **OR** a gingerbread house?

a house of mirrors **OR** a house of sofa cushions?

YOU MUST CHOOSE!

135

CHAPTER SEVEN

WOULD YOU...

Sometimes, simple "yes" or "no" questions aren't so simple. See if you have the guts (or the stupidity) to take on this chapter's challenges. Would you...? Could you...? Should you...? Only you can decide.

Would you... let a mad scientist surgically attach a giant crab claw to you in place of your right hand to have front row seats to the sports team of your choice for the rest of your life?

Would you... wear your grandmother's clothes to get an extra $50 per week allowance?

Would you... clean a gassy elephant's backside for $5,000?

YOU MUST CHOOSE!

Would you... never cut your hair again for $100,000?

Would you... never cut your fingernails again for $1,000,000?

Things to think about: typing, picking your nose

Would you... drink a glass of semi-frozen snot for $2,000?

YOU MUST CHOOSE!

Would you... step in dog doo on purpose in your bare feet for $50?

Would you... go to school seven days a week if you never had to do any homework?

Would you... give up shoes to be a famous singer?

YOU MUST CHOOSE!

Would you... eat a dozen live caterpillars if your parents had to do whatever you wanted for three days? How about 100 caterpillars in one sitting if they had to do what you wanted for a month?

Would you... permanently chain a penguin to your leg for $100,000? How would this affect your life? Your dating life? Playing tennis, etc.?

Would you... legally change your name to Chewbacca if you were guaranteed a successful career as a professional tennis player?

YOU MUST CHOOSE!

Would you... Krazy Glue your pinky and ring finger together for two days for $250?

Would you... Krazy Glue your palms together for a day for $2,000?

Would you... Krazy glue your shoes onto your feet for $5,000?

YOU MUST CHOOSE!

Would you... give up dessert for five years to be able to dunk?

Would you... never change your underwear again to be Vice President of the United States?

Would you... bite into a block of ice with your front teeth for $150?

YOU MUST CHOOSE!

Would you... eat a stranger's boogers if it meant you'd get straight A's?

Would you... swim a lap in a pool of maggots for $10,000?

Would you... surgically attach a permanent handlebar mustache onto your face to never get sunburn?

YOU MUST CHOOSE!

Would you... live in an igloo for a year if you never again had to do chores?

Would you... replace your bed with a bed of nails to have the artistic skills of Picasso?

Would you... give up all junk food for the rest of your life for the opportunity to go to outer space?

YOU MUST CHOOSE!

145

Would you... never leave your room again to have the power to see into the future?

Would you... wear your underwear on the outside of your pants to have a comic book series based on your life?

Would you... want to weigh 800 pounds if you could live until you were 200 years old? How long would you want to live?

YOU MUST CHOOSE!

Would you... consume 100 bananas in one sitting to be able to throw a 90mph fastball?

Would you... want to be invisible between the hours of 2pm and 3pm each day?

Would you... wear a kilt all the time to be able to speak six different languages fluently?

YOU MUST CHOOSE!

Would you... try to hold in your poops for two weeks for a free round-trip ticket anywhere in the world (If you fail, you get nothing)?

Would you... permanently affix Vulcan ears onto your head to be 25% more popular?

Would you... limit your TV to *Dora the Explorer* for the next 5 years for $10,000?

YOU MUST CHOOSE!

Would you... eat a cow brain and mayo sandwich for $5,000?

Would you... slam your thumb with a hammer as hard as you could to never again sweat?

Would you... give up the ability to control your bladder to have the ability to fly?
Things to think about: the people below you

YOU MUST CHOOSE!

149

Would you... trade your house with your best friend's?

Would you... give up video games for world peace?

Would you... eat a live worm, calf eyeball, this book, a hair sandwich, and a bowl of lice for $1,000 and an autographed photo of Kobe Bryant?

YOU MUST CHOOSE!

Would you... trade your family pet for a brand new game each week for a year?

Would you... change your name to "Lumpkins" for $50,000?

YOU MUST CHOOSE!

151

CHAPTER EIGHT

Getting Personal

It's time to get personal. For the questions in this chapter, you may need to fill a blank with the name of a friend. Or maybe the name of an enemy. Don't blame us for this chapter. It's your warped mind that's responsible for these deranged dilemmas.

Would you rather...

have to sit next to _____
(insert annoying person)

OR

_____ in every class?
(insert smelly person)

Would you rather...

have _____ as your parents
(insert two mean teachers)

OR

_____ as a brother?
(insert a bully)

YOU MUST CHOOSE!

154

Would you rather...

have to use _____'s dirty clothes as a
(insert disgusting person)
bath towel

OR

drink a cup of _____'s sweat?
(insert another disgusting person)

Reasons 1st choice is better

....
....
....
....

Reasons 2nd choice is better

....
....
....
....

YOU MUST CHOOSE!

Would you rather...

be as popular as _____
(insert most popular person you know)

OR

have sports skills greater than _____ ?
(insert best athlete in school you know)

Would you rather...

eat a baked beans dinner with _____
(insert someone with lots of gas)

OR

have a long, fine four course meal with

_____ ?
(insert horribly mean or annoying person)

YOU MUST CHOOSE!

Would you rather...

be the personal assistant for _____
(insert sports star)

OR

the personal assistant for _____ ?
(insert famous actor)

Would you rather...

kiss _____ on the lips
(insert unappealing person)

OR

kiss _____ 's butt?
(insert friend)

YOU MUST CHOOSE!

157

Would you rather...

marry _____
(insert person with awful personality)

OR

_____ ?
(insert nerd)

Would you rather...

take a deep minute-long whiff of _____'s
(insert gross person)
gym socks

OR

use the bathroom right after _____
(insert gross person)

was just in there for fifteen minutes?

YOU MUST CHOOSE!

Would you rather...

lick _____ 's armpit
    (insert gross person)

OR

lick a _____ 's _____ ?
      (insert animal)   (insert body part)

Would you rather...

have _____ do all your homework
     (insert smart person)

OR

go out with _____ ?
              (insert attractive person)

YOU MUST CHOOSE!

Would you rather...

be able to access the Web from your

_____

(insert something you currently have in your backpack or pocket)

OR

be able to make phone calls using your _____ ?

(insert part of the body)

Would you rather get into a fight with...

_____

(insert friend you could beat up)

OR

_____ ?

(insert enemy who is bigger than you)

YOU MUST CHOOSE!

Would you... eat a pizza covered in

pepperoni and _____ in exchange

(insert something disgusting)

for two floor tickets to a _____ concert?

(insert your favorite band)

Would you rather...

only be able to chew gum previously chewed by

_____

(insert friend who never brushes his teeth)

OR

use Kleenex previously used by _____ ?

(insert friend with severe allergies)

YOU MUST CHOOSE!

Would you rather...

be locked up in a 5' by 5' room for a month with

_____
(insert extremely talkative acquaintance)

OR

_____ ?
(insert disgusting person)

Take a vote!

Number of people who voted for choice #1:.........

Number of people who voted for choice #2:.........

YOU MUST CHOOSE!

Would you rather...

have the face of _____
(insert actor/actress)

OR

the IQ of _____ ?
(insert really smart person)

Who chose what and why...

Name _____ Choice _____

Why _____

Name _____ Choice _____

Why _____

Name _____ Choice _____

Why _____

YOU MUST CHOOSE!

Would you rather...

be limited to wearing one article of clothing for the rest of your life: a _____
(insert article of clothing)

OR

eating one food: _____ ?
(insert food)

Would you rather...

have a free, lifetime supply of _____
(insert your favorite snack)

OR

have a new episode of _____ to watch once each day?
(insert your favorite television show)

YOU MUST CHOOSE!

Would you rather...

appear as _____ in all photographs
                (insert cartoon character)

OR

sound like _____ on all recordings?
              (insert person)

Take a vote!

Number of people who voted for **choice #1**:.........

Number of people who voted for **choice #2**:.........

YOU MUST CHOOSE!

Would you... be unable to

_____ in exchange for
(insert one of the five senses)

being a first-round draft pick in _____?
(insert your favorite sport)

Would you rather...

have a weekend trip to _____
(insert place you've always wanted to go)

OR

get to have _____ over for dinner?
(insert celebrity)

YOU MUST CHOOSE!

Would you rather...

have _____ be your date to a school dance
(insert favorite celebrity)

OR

_____ be your team's coach?
(insert favorite athlete)

Reasons *1st choice* is better

....
....
....
....
....

Reasons *2nd choice* is better

....
....
....
....
....

YOU MUST CHOOSE!

CHAPTER NINE

Doubly Doubly Disgusting

Turns out there's something worse than doubly disgusting: doubly doubly disgusting! If you've been brushing up on your math, you'll realize that this means the bugs are four times as nasty, the guts are four times as gruesome, the boogers are four times as big, and the smells are four times as smelly! And remember, "I can't choose" is not an option.

Would you rather...

drink a glass of ten-month-old moldy milk, feeling every warm chunk as it slides down your throat

OR

eat a cereal bowl of caterpillars with a spoon, feeling the guts forcefully squirt into your mouth as you bite down?

YOU MUST CHOOSE!

Would you rather...

have noses protruding from all over your body

OR

have 6 foot long armpit hair?

Reasons **1st choice** is better

Reasons **2nd choice** is better

Would you rather...

have to wear live spider earrings

OR

have a hairy mole that wanders all over your face?

YOU MUST CHOOSE!

Would you rather...

be eating an apple only to find a wriggling worm in it

OR

be eating an orange only to find maggots in it?

Would you rather...

suck the pus out of 20 zits

OR

chew on a handful of recently removed warts?

YOU MUST CHOOSE!

Would you rather...

have to use a used diaper as a book bag

OR

wear a shirt made of used tissues?

Would you rather...

use peanut butter as deodorant

OR

as toothpaste and not be able to rinse?

YOU MUST CHOOSE!

Would you rather...

have a skunk shoot its smelly spray straight into your nostrils

OR

have to sleep in the back of a garbage truck for a week?

Would you rather...

drink a full cup of sweat with a straw

OR

without one?

YOU MUST CHOOSE!

Would you rather...

bathe in a tub of bloodworms

OR

drink a bloodworm smoothie?

Would you rather...

cough up a hairball like a cat

OR

be swallowed and coughed up like a hairball by a giant cat?

YOU MUST CHOOSE!

Would you rather...

let a tarantula crawl all over your body for two minutes

OR

drop a live fish into your pants?

Would you rather...

your bathroom faucets produce hot tar rather than water

OR

have to use bug guts as shampoo?

YOU MUST CHOOSE!

OULD YOU RATHER...
HAVE GRANOLA BOOGERS

R HAVE CHERRY-FLAVORED EAR WAX?

Would you rather...

have to subsist entirely by eating live insects

OR

by eating flowers?

Would you rather...

dive into a pool of mayo **OR** honey?

mucus **OR** thumbtacks?

rats **OR** glass shards?

YOU MUST CHOOSE!

Would you rather...

put on a helmet filled with earwigs

OR

sleep in a bed filled with leeches?

Would you rather...

fart the smell of lavender

OR

belch the sound of church bells?

YOU MUST CHOOSE!

179

Would you rather...

get caught in a rainstorm of bird-doo

OR

a hailstorm of boogers?

Would you rather...

receive 1,000 sloppy wet kisses from random grandmas and grandpas

OR

be spit-up on by 200 random babies?

YOU MUST CHOOSE!

Would you rather...

eat a taco full of beetles

OR

eat a cud that has been chewed by a cow for five minutes and then spit out?

Would you rather...

be sneezed on by ten giraffes

OR

farted on by a rhino?

YOU MUST CHOOSE!

Would you rather...

have thorn-covered skin

OR

a single unremovable 3-foot long hair sprouting from the tip of your nose?

Reasons **1st choice** is better

....
....
....
....
....

Reasons **2nd choice** is better

....
....
....
....
....

YOU MUST CHOOSE!

182

Would you rather...

sneeze through your butt

OR

fart through your nose?

Would you rather...

reach between the couch cushions and eat whatever you find

OR

eat 1,000 lima beans?

YOU MUST CHOOSE!

Would you rather...

be able to eat food only from the garbage

OR

only be able to eat pet food?

Would you rather...

find out the black licorice you just ate was actually a really, really thick armpit hair

OR

that the gobstobber you just put into your mouth was a sheep's eyeball?

YOU MUST CHOOSE!

Would you rather...

have to "mow" a lawn by chomping on the grass with your mouth

OR

have to "sponge" the cafeteria tables with your tongue?

Who chose what and why...

Name _____ Choice _____

Why _____

Name _____ Choice _____

Why _____

Name _____ Choice _____

Why _____

YOU MUST CHOOSE!

Would you rather...

lick a cheese grater

OR

a toilet plunger?

Would you rather...

slide under your covers, only to discover a dozen roaches scurrying about

OR

sit on the toilet, only to discover a rat swimming around?

YOU MUST CHOOSE!

WOULD YOU RATHER... CAUSE 4.0 MAGNITUDE EARTHQUAKES EVERY TIME YOU FART

OR GENERATE A CATEGORY ONE HURRICANE EVERY TIME YOU SNEEZE?

Would you rather...

have squid tentacles for hair

OR

have an anteater's nose?

Would you rather...

drink a glass of blended poison ivy

OR

have your eyeballs pecked away slowly by hungry crows?

YOU MUST CHOOSE!

189

Would you rather...

have all of your teeth fall out

OR

all your hair and fingernails fall off?

Would you rather...

be reincarnated as a dung beetle

OR

a gnat?

YOU MUST CHOOSE!

Would you rather...

have to put raw chopped meat in your breakfast cereal

OR

in your underwear?

Would you rather...

only be allowed to drink other people's backwash

OR

only be able to eat rotten, moldy food?

YOU MUST CHOOSE!

Would you rather...

have a pimple inside your nose

OR

on your eyelid?

Take a vote!

Number of people who voted for **choice #1**:.........

Number of people who voted for **choice #2**:.........

YOU MUST CHOOSE!

CHAPTER TEN

RANDOM PLAY

Would You Rather...? is on random play. And when we say "random," we mean really RANDOM! There's no telling what kind of question will be asked: a curse, a torture, a power? And there's no limit to the dauntingly disgusting situations you might be faced with.

Would you rather...

have a perfect memory but speak with a pirate accent

OR

be great at miniature golf but walk with a "pooped your pants" walk?

Would you rather...

have one foot twice as large as the other

OR

one arm six inches longer than the other? How about one foot three feet longer than the other or one arm seven feet longer than the other?

YOU MUST CHOOSE!

Would you rather...

have to wear all your clothing inside out

OR

have to plug yourself in every few hours to recharge before you shut down like a laptop computer?

Take a vote!

Number of people who voted for **choice #1**:.........

Number of people who voted for **choice #2**:.........

YOU MUST CHOOSE!

WOULD YOU RATHER...HAVE A SMALL THUNDERSTORM PERPETUALLY OVERHEAD

OR HAVE A CATCHERS MASK PERMANENTLY AFFIXED TO YOUR HEAD?

Would you rather...

your ears and big toes switch places

OR

your nose and belly button?

Would you rather...

spend a year not talking to your family

OR

not talking to your friends?

YOU MUST CHOOSE!

Would you rather...

have the power to correctly answer the questions on your tests by stuffing the test down your pants

OR

go to a school where your only tests are on sports statistics and trivia?

Reasons *1st choice* is better

....

....

....

....

....

Reasons *2nd choice* is better

....

....

....

....

....

YOU MUST CHOOSE!

WOULD YOU RATHER...
HAVE A GIRAFFE CHAINED TO YOUR LEG FOR A MONTH

ABC

OR HAVE TO SLEEP IN A CRIB FOR THE REST YOUR LIFE?

DAILY NEWS

Would you rather...

only be able to greet people by yodeling

OR

by giving a devastating noogie instead of shaking hands?

Would you rather...

have taste buds all over your body

OR

functioning clock hands on your face?

YOU MUST CHOOSE!

Would you rather live in a world where....

babies were born with a mute button

OR

parents were?

Take a vote!

Number of people who voted for choice #1:.........

Number of people who voted for choice #2:.........

YOU MUST CHOOSE!

WOULD YOU RATHER... HAVE THE LETTERS ON YOUR KEYBOARD RANDOMLY CHANGE EVERY DAY

OR ONLY BE ABLE TO TYPE WITH YOUR TONGUE?

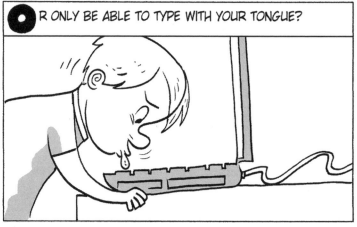

Would you rather...

never be able to wash your hands

OR

never be able to brush your teeth?

Would you rather...

have feet covered in thick fur

OR

bright red irises?

YOU MUST CHOOSE!

Would you rather...

have little creatures inside your mouth that clean your teeth

OR

have nostrils that dispense mustard and ketchup when you blow your nose?

Would you rather...

live in a world where people's heights changed from day to day

OR

where their ages did?

YOU MUST CHOOSE!

Would you rather...

always have to wear a twenty pound necklace

OR

always have to wear a snowboard?

Who chose what and why...

Name _____ Choice _____

Why _____

Name _____ Choice _____

Why _____

Name _____ Choice _____

Why _____

YOU MUST CHOOSE!

WOULD YOU RATHER...
WALK LIKE YOUR GRANDMOTHER

OR HAVE HER WARDROBE?

Would you rather...

have five elbows on each arm

OR

one elbow on each arm the size of a bowling ball?

Would you rather...

your skin be made of felt **OR** plastic wrap?

stone **OR** bark?

omelet **OR** glass?

YOU MUST CHOOSE!

CHAPTER ELEVEN

MAKE YOUR OWN QUESTIONS!

Okay, so you should have the hang of it by now. But do you have what it takes to write your own *Would You Rather...?* questions? Here's a hint: When in doubt, think weird, gross, embarrassing, cool, or painful. And don't worry; not only are there no wrong answers—in this case, there are no wrong questions!

Make Your Own "DISGUSTING" Question!
Make up two choices that are equally disgusting!

Would you rather...

_____

_____

OR

_____

_____ ?

Who chose what and why...

Name _____ Choice _____

Why _____

Name _____ Choice _____

Why _____

Name _____ Choice _____

Why _____

Make Your Own "DISGUSTING" Question!

Make up **two choices** that are **equally disgusting!**

Would you rather...

_____

_____

OR

_____

_____?

Who chose what and why...

Name _____ Choice _____

Why _____

Name _____ Choice _____

Why _____

Name _____ Choice _____

Why _____

Make Your Own "DISGUSTING" Question!
Make up **two choices** that are **equally disgusting!**

Would you rather...

_ _ _ _ _ _ _ _ _ _ _ _ _ _ _ _ _ _ _

_ _ _ _ _ _ _ _ _ _ _ _ _ _ _ _ _ _ _

OR

_ _ _ _ _ _ _ _ _ _ _ _ _ _ _ _ _ _ _

_ _ _ _ _ _ _ _ _ _ _ _ _ _ _ _ _ _ _ ?

Who chose what and why...

Name _____ Choice _____
Why _____
Name _____ Choice _____
Why _____
Name _____ Choice _____
Why _____

Make Your Own "DISGUSTING" Question!
Make up **two choices** that are **equally disgusting!**

Would you rather...

_____

_____

OR

_____

_____ ?

Who chose what and why...

Name	Choice
Why	
Name	Choice
Why	
Name	Choice
Why	

Make Your Own "PUNISHMENTS" Question!

Would you rather...

_____

_____

OR

_____

_____?

Who chose what and why...

Name _____ Choice _____

Why _____

Name _____ Choice _____

Why _____

Name _____ Choice _____

Why _____

Make Your Own "FANTASY" Question!

Would you rather...

_____

_____

OR

_____

_____ ?

Who chose what and why...

Name _____ Choice _____

Why _____

Name _____ Choice _____

Why _____

Name _____ Choice _____

Why _____

Make Your Own "POWERS" Question!

Would you rather...

_____

_____

OR

_____

_____?

Who chose what and why...

Name _____ Choice _____

Why _____

Name _____ Choice _____

Why _____

Name _____ Choice _____

Why _____

Make Your Own "CURSES" Question!

Would you rather...

_____

_____

OR

_____

_____ ?

Who chose what and why...

Name _____ Choice _____

Why _____

Name _____ Choice _____

Why _____

Name _____ Choice _____

Why _____

Make Your Own "DISGUSTING" Question!
Make up two choices that are equally disgusting!

Would you rather...

_____

_____

OR

_____

_____?

Who chose what and why...

Name _____ Choice _____

Why _____

Name _____ Choice _____

Why _____

Name _____ Choice _____

Why _____

Would You Rather...? Gross-out

The original collection of dementedly disgusting questions, *Would You Rather...? Gross-Out* features hundreds of devilish dilemmas and imaginative illustrations. You'll crack up as you ponder questions like:

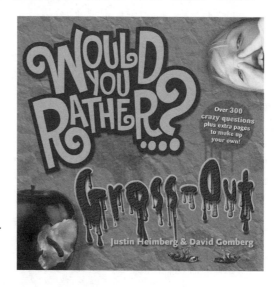

Would you rather...
have a tape-dispensing mouth
OR
a bottle-opening nostril?

About the Authors:

Little is known about authors Justin Heimberg and David Gomberg. Some say they are locked up in a mental institution where they spend all day writing bizarre questions on their cells' walls. Others say they are aliens determined to confuse the planet into chaos. Still others say they are stricken with a bad case of "diarrhea of the imagination" for which no sort of toilet paper has yet been invented. If the last theory is right, look out! They say it's contagious!